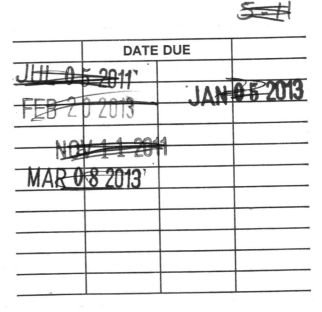

"In a world filled with hate, we must still dare to hope. In a world filled with anger, we must still dare to comfort. In a world filled with despair, we must still dare to dream. And in a world filled with distrust, we must still dare to believe."

Michael Jackson

1958–2009

ABDO
Publishing Company

Michael Jackson

KING OF POP

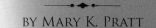

by Mary K. Pratt

4-11
35 26

CREDITS

Published by ABDO Publishing Company, 8000 West 78th Street, Edina, Minnesota 55439. Copyright © 2010 by Abdo Consulting Group, Inc. International copyrights reserved in all countries. No part of this book may be reproduced in any form without written permission from the publisher. The Essential Library™ is a trademark and logo of ABDO Publishing Company.

Printed in the United States of America,
North Mankato, Minnesota.
012010
062010

♻ PRINTED ON RECYCLED PAPER

Editor: Rebecca Rowell
Copy Editor: Paula Lewis
Interior Design and Production: Kazuko Collins
Cover Design: Becky Daum

Library of Congress Cataloging-in-Publication Data
Pratt, Mary K.
  Michael Jackson : king of pop / Mary K. Pratt.
      p. cm. — (Lives cut short)
  Includes bibliographical references.
  ISBN 978-1-60453-788-8
  1. Jackson, Michael, 1958-2009. 2. Rock musicians—United States—Biography—Juvenile literature. I. Title.

  ML420.J175P73 2010
  782.42166092—dc22
  [B]
                                    2009034355

TABLE OF CONTENTS

1

A Dazzling Performer

t was a special performance in the spring of 1983. The famous singing group the Jackson 5 had reunited onstage. The thrilled audience applauded enthusiastically. The brothers performed a medley of some of their biggest hits, including "I Want You Back" and "I'll Be There."

After wrapping up their performance, the brothers smiled and waved to the audience. They hugged each other and four of the brothers exited the stage, leaving only one Jackson—Michael—alone in the spotlight.

▶ MICHAEL JACKSON ENTERTAINED AUDIENCES WITH HIS SINGING AND DANCING.

"I like those songs a lot," he told the audience, "but especially I like the new songs."[1] Jackson stopped briefly, standing motionless on the stage—a solitary figure in front of a microphone in a white spotlight. The drumbeat started, steady and strong. He swiftly moved his right hand up from his side and effortlessly put on a black fedora hat. One quick move, and then he was still again. The anticipation continued to build.

The crowd cheered, and people jumped to their feet as the music to Jackson's hit song "Billie Jean" began. Jackson, slender and nimble, started to dance, feet tapping and hips thrusting to the beat. His black jacket, silver shirt, and silver socks—all sequined—sparkled in the bright lights. One glove, worn on his left hand, flashed in the spotlight as he moved. The sight was dazzling, but it was Jackson's singing and dancing that astounded the audience.

Jackson hooked the audience from the start and never let up. But as good

The Magic of Motown

Motown not only launched the Jackson 5 in the late 1960s but was essential in introducing U.S. audiences to many other black singers and musicians. Berry Gordy started Motown in January 1959. A former boxer and automotive worker, Gordy also had experience as a songwriter and a record store owner. He proved that he had a keen eye for talent by signing legendary performers such as Smokey Robinson and the Miracles, the Temptations, the Four Tops, Diana Ross and the Supremes, Gladys Knight and the Pips, Stevie Wonder, and Marvin Gaye.

as the opening was, there was more to come. Halfway through his nearly five-minute solo performance, Jackson amazed the audience. He twirled, hitched up his black pants, and unleashed a move that stunned the crowd and started a trend: the moonwalk. He glided backward, although his feet looked as though they were simultaneously moving forward. He twirled again, and ended *en pointe*, resting on the tips of his black loafer-like shoes for a second that seemed to stop time. He then began to dance again.

HOMECOMING

Nearly 50 million people watched Jackson's performance for the television special to celebrate the twenty-fifth anniversary of Motown Records. The special, *Motown 25: Yesterday, Today and Forever*, was broadcast on NBC on May 16, 1983. It had been taped about a month earlier before a live audience. The event was something of a homecoming for the young performer.

Was There a Real Billie Jean?

The song "Billie Jean" tells the story of a woman accusing a man of fathering her child and about the man denying a relationship with her. Such powerful lyrics led to speculation about whether a real woman inspired the tale. Jackson denied this in his 1988 autobiography, *Moonwalk*. "The girl in the song is a composite of people we've been plagued by over the years. This kind of thing happened to some of my brothers and I used to be really amazed by it," he said.[2]

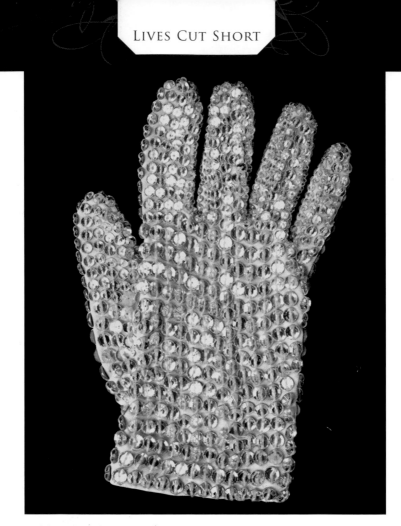

▲ MICHAEL JACKSON'S TRADEMARK WAS WEARING A
SEQUINED GLOVE ONLY ON ONE HAND.

The 24-year-old singer had gotten his start with
the legendary Detroit, Michigan, recording
company. He had signed a contract with
Motown in 1968. At the time, he was only ten
years old and part of the Jackson 5, his family's
singing group.

Jackson and four of his brothers rocketed to
fame in the late 1960s and 1970s. Michael was

the youngest member of the quintet, and he was almost always front and center as the group's lead singer. His strong singing voice, charismatic onstage presence, and fancy footwork brought the group several hit singles and sold-out concert tours.

But by the time of this performance in spring 1983, Jackson had launched a solo career, and his star was rising to new heights. Following the release of his album *Thriller* the previous year, Jackson was gaining exposure and popularity.

When the Motown special was being planned, the Jackson 5 was asked to perform. Jackson initially declined the offer to appear with his brothers. He preferred making music videos and acting in film, where he could perfect his performance. Jackson had worked hard to build his career as a solo artist. He was creating his own musical sound and style that would set him apart from his siblings in fans' minds. Jackson feared that performing on the Motown special might undo all of his hard solo work.

The Moonwalk

The moonwalk became a signature move for Michael Jackson, but many others performed the dance step before Jackson made it famous. The move had developed out on the streets as part of the then-popular break-dance style. Jackson rehearsed it privately before realizing he could incorporate it into his act—ultimately making it his own.

But family members and Motown founder Berry Gordy pressured Michael Jackson to take part in the celebration. Michael's father thought his son's success as a solo artist might help the Jackson 5 regain their popularity. Jackson relented, but only after he earned one concession—he could perform his hit song after singing with his brothers as part of the Jackson 5. It would be the only non-Motown number in the show.

Once Michael signed on to perform, he and his brothers came together just as they had when they were younger. The five siblings practiced and rehearsed in the family home in

The Gloved One

Although Jackson had worn a single glove prior to his album *Thriller*, his decision to sport a white glittery glove on his left hand during the Motown 25 show created a look that would define his image for the rest of his life.

Jackson, nicknamed "the Gloved One" after the performance, said he thought "wearing one glove was cool. Wearing two gloves seemed so ordinary."[3]

He also seemed surprised by the widespread reaction to his single gloved hand following his 1983 performance. "I actually had been wearing the glove for a long time, but it hadn't gotten a lot of attention until all of a sudden it hit with *Thriller* in 1983," he said.[4]

The single, sparkling white glove appeared to be nothing more than a fashion statement from the superstar, but some have speculated that Jackson actually wore the glove due to one or more of his medical conditions. Later in his life, Jackson said he had vitiligo, a skin disease that causes blotches of lightening skin.

▲ YEARS BEFORE HE BECAME POPULAR AS A SOLO ARTIST, MICHAEL JACKSON, *CENTER*, ACHIEVED FAME WITH HIS BROTHERS AS PART OF THE JACKSON 5.

Encino, California, for hours in preparation for the reunion performance. They videotaped their rehearsals to review and critique their work.

Because he was busy practicing with his brothers, Michael did not spend as much time as he would have liked planning his own performance. He had asked assistants to get him a black hat, but he did not know how he would use it in his act. Instead, he left much of that preparation until the night before the show was to be taped. He figured out what he wanted to do for his solo act and managed to create his dazzling performance in a short amount of time.

Jackson's decision to appear on the Motown special proved to be a good one. His performance of "Billie Jean" that spring became one of the most celebrated appearances of his decades-long career. "I'll never forget that night, because when I opened my eyes at the end, people were on their feet applauding. I was overwhelmed by the reaction. It felt so good," Jackson later stated.[5]

Jackson's performance was one of the most memorable of the evening. *Rolling Stone* magazine called his routine "the most electrifying five minutes of the evening."[6]

Michael Jackson's star was shooting toward the stratosphere. His name, face, and music would soon be known worldwide.

—— • ◆ • ——

Astaire Approves

Jackson's performance at the Motown 25 celebration impressed Fred Astaire, another important performer. Astaire, a Broadway stage and film star known for his singing and dancing talents throughout the twentieth century, called Jackson the day after the show aired on television. Jackson remembered Astaire's compliments. The veteran performer told the young singer he had given a great performance at the Motown special. Astaire even compared Jackson's style to his own, telling Jackson, "You're an angry dancer. I'm the same way. I used to do the same thing with my cane."[7]

▲ MICHAEL JACKSON IN THE EARLY 1980S, WHEN HIS SOLO
CAREER WAS JUST TAKING OFF

2

GROWING UP
JACKSON

Michael Joseph Jackson was born on August 29, 1958, in Gary, Indiana. He was the seventh of Joseph "Joe" and Katherine Jackson's nine children. The large Jackson family lived in a small, two-bedroom house located in part of an all-black neighborhood in the midwestern industrial city. "Our family's house in Gary was tiny, only three rooms really, but at the time it seemed much larger to me," Michael said.[1]

The family had barely enough money to get by. Joe worked as a crane operator at a nearby

steel mill. Katherine occasionally worked part-time at a department store to earn money for family necessities.

By all accounts, Joe Jackson was a tough father. He decided what happened in his home, and he expected his children to obey everything he said. He regularly hit them when they did not do what they were told. Joe kept his children from playing with other children in the neighborhood, and he did not allow them to hang out with friends outside of school. Not surprisingly, the Jackson children were afraid of their father. Because Katherine did not want her children raised in a divorced home, she tolerated such behavior in order to keep her marriage and family together.

MUSICAL BEGINNINGS

At first glance, the Jackson clan might seem an unlikely source of musical genius. But Joe and Katherine

---

The Jackson Family

There were six boys and three girls in the Jackson family:

- Maureen (Rebbie), born May 29, 1950
- Sigmund Esco (Jackie), born May 4, 1951
- Tariano Adaryl (sometimes spelled Toriano) (Tito), born October 15, 1953
- Jermaine LaJuane, born December 11, 1954
- LaToya Yvonne, born May 29, 1956
- Marlon David, born March 12, 1957
- Michael Joseph, born August 29, 1958
- Steven Randall (Randy), born October 29, 1961
- Janet Dameta, May 16, 1966

Katherine actually gave birth to ten children. In 1957, she had twins, but one of the babies—Marlon's twin—died within a day of birth.

▲ THE JACKSON FAMILY IN 1975 (NOT PICTURED: REBBIE)

both had dreamed of careers in music. Joe was part of a rhythm and blues (R & B) band, the Falcons, which he formed with his brother and four friends. The group performed some of the popular hits of the day—songs by Chuck Berry, Otis Redding, and Little Richard. The band's gigs at local clubs brought additional income into the household.

Katherine was from Alabama and grew up listening to country-western music. She played the clarinet and the piano, and she was a talented singer. But as a child, she contracted polio. The disease left her unable to walk without crutches or braces for much of her childhood. And though she learned to walk without those aids, polio left her with a limp. Katherine also missed a good portion of her schooling while growing up. Due to her challenging childhood, it is not surprising that she abandoned her dream of becoming a performer.

Joe and Katherine tried to teach their children what they knew about music. The couple's musical influence on their children was significant. The elder Jacksons also encouraged their children to learn from others. They paid for music classes for the oldest two children, Rebbie and Jackie, while the others had music lessons through their schools. Some of Michael's earliest memories were of his mother singing songs such as

"When you're a show business child, you really don't have the maturity to understand a great deal of what is going on around you. People make a lot of decisions concerning your life when you're out of the room. So here's what I remember. I remember singing at the top of my voice and dancing with real joy and working too hard for a child. Of course, there are many details I don't remember at all. I do remember the Jackson 5 really taking off when I was only eight or nine."[2]
—*Michael Jackson*

▲ JOE AND KATHERINE JACKSON'S MUSICAL INTERESTS INFLUENCED THEIR CHILDREN.

"You Are My Sunshine" and "Cotton Fields." The children also had plenty of exposure to R & B standards when Joe's group held regular practice sessions in the family's tiny living room.

PROVING THEY ARE MUSICIANS

Joe Jackson took his music seriously, as well as his guitar. He stored his prized instrument in his bedroom closet and warned his children that the instrument was off-limits. "No one was to touch the guitar while he was out. Period," Michael remembered. "Therefore, Jackie, Tito, and Jermaine were careful to see that Mom was in the kitchen when they 'borrowed' the guitar."[3]

But the guitar proved too tempting for Tito. He had learned to play the saxophone in school and was quick to learn the guitar after seeing his father play it so often. Tito, along with Jackie and Jermaine, practiced the scales they learned in school and songs they heard on the radio. The boys played until they figured out the right notes and chords.

Joe caught on to what the boys were doing when he came home and found one of the guitar's strings broken.

Music Kept the Jacksons Safe

Gary, Indiana, was a tough industrial city in the 1960s, when the Jackson children were growing up. Factory work made up much of the available work at the time, although unemployment was high.

The city's neighborhoods, including the Jacksons', were primarily working-class sections. And although the Jacksons' street consisted of well-kept, modest homes at the time, Gary also had a tougher side. Joe and Katherine knew there were neighborhood gangs who tried to recruit young boys the same age as some of their sons. The couple worried that one of their children could be hurt in the streets.

Keeping their children safe was one reason Joe and Katherine Jackson allowed their children to attend the rehearsals Joe held with the Falcons in the family's living room. Safety also figured into the Jackson parents' decision to encourage their children's musical interests. The couple figured that if their children were at home working toward a goal, they would be safer from trouble.

Joe dealt a harsh punishment to Tito for breaking the string. Crying, Tito told his father that he really could play the instrument.

Katherine came to her son's defense. "The boys are good, Joseph. I mean they are really good," she told him. So Joe issued a challenge to Tito: "OK, let me see what you can do."[4]

Tito proved to his father that he had a special talent for the guitar. In return, Joe encouraged his son's interest. One day, Joe came home from work with a red electric guitar for Tito with orders to practice.

Joe started teaching Tito songs and later bought Jermaine a bass guitar. He put Jackie, Tito, and Jermaine together to rehearse, often for hours a day. Marlon and Michael watched and absorbed the music lessons that Joe was giving their older brothers. Marlon soon joined in, playing bongos and singing.

It was not long before Michael became part of the family act. Initially, he played along on

Other Band Members

The Jackson boys were not the only members of the Jacksons' act in the early days. Sisters Rebbie and LaToya would play violin and clarinet, although both later dropped out of the lineup. Meanwhile, Joe Jackson recruited musicians from outside the family to join the group. Johnny Jackson played drums. Ronnie Rancifer played keyboard. They departed the band much later, however, leaving just the five oldest Jackson brothers.

the bongos. Joe was grooming Jermaine to be lead singer. But one day, Katherine watched little Michael singing along to a James Brown song. Katherine instantly saw something special in Michael's performance, although he was only about five years old. She recognized the power of his voice and his dancing abilities, even at his young age. She told Joe as soon as he arrived home from work that the group should have Michael as a lead singer. Michael's addition rounded out the family's musical lineup, creating what would become the Jackson 5.

Michael's First Solo Performance

Michael Jackson's first live performance as a solo artist came well before his recording career. It also came before his family's band took off. When Michael was in first grade at Garnett School, he participated in a school program. He sang "Climb Every Mountain," an uplifting number from the musical *The Sound of Music*. He chose the piece with the help of his parents. His stirring performance earned him a standing ovation from the audience and left some of his teachers in tears.

▲ MICHAEL JACKSON, *FRONT RIGHT,* AND HIS BROTHERS
FORMED THE MUSICAL GROUP THE JACKSON 5.

3

THE RISE OF THE JACKSON 5

From its start, Joe Jackson saw potential in his sons' band, the Jackson 5. He believed their musical talent could make them stars, and he soon started planning a strategy to put them in the spotlight. He bought instruments, microphones, and amplifiers instead of the necessities his family needed. Although his decision caused many arguments with Katherine, Joe saw these purchases as investments in the children's futures.

▸ THE APOLLO THEATER IN HARLEM, NEW YORK CITY

PRACTICING AND PERFORMING

The boys' lives were filled with music. Joe would spend several hours in the afternoons and evenings watching his children rehearse and critiquing their performance. He taught them some of the popular songs of that era—hits such as "My Girl" by the Temptations. These rehearsals gave Michael time to sharpen his talents. He learned singing techniques from Jermaine and dance moves from Marlon.

Although the boys enjoyed playing and performing, their rehearsals were tough. Joe was strict, sometimes hitting the children if they did not perform to his standards. The hours they spent practicing also left little time for playing. Neighborhood children sometimes teased them for spending so much time indoors. Michael was occasionally lonely, and he sometimes wished he could be like other children.

After a short time, Joe Jackson felt his boys were ready to perform publicly. By 1964, he started entering his sons in talent contests. They

"My father did always protect us and that's no small feat. He always tried to make sure people didn't cheat us. He looked after our interests in the best ways. He might have made a few mistakes along the way, but he always thought he was doing what was right for his family. And, of course, most of what my father helped us accomplish was wonderful and unique."[1]
—*Michael Jackson*

easily won many of them. The boys often performed under the name the Ripples and Waves Plus Michael. They later performed as the Jackson Brothers. The group took the top prize at Gary's citywide talent competition, held in the Roosevelt High School gym. The Jacksons performed "My Girl," with Jermaine singing lead vocals. They followed it up with the song "Barefootin'," which featured Michael dancing barefoot around the stage.

The Jacksons also started performing at places other than talent shows. They played their first paying gig in the summer of 1964 at a discount store. By 1966, Joe was booking them at nightclubs in and around Gary and Chicago, Illinois, which was less than an hour's drive away. Soon, the band—now called the Jackson 5—toured theaters and clubs throughout the country that featured black entertainers. Many of the clubs where the boys performed were home to adult entertainment, often featuring strippers and comics as well as musicians.

Early Influences on Michael Jackson

In addition to his father's rhythm and blues band, the Falcons, Michael Jackson's early musical influences included a mix of R & B performers, soul singers, and funk bands. Musicians who made an impression on Michael included Jackie Wilson, the Temptations, the Isley Brothers, Marvin Gaye, Stevie Wonder, Joe Tex, James Brown, Wilson Pickett, and Sly & the Family Stone.

The Jackson 5 became a regular act at Mr. Lucky's, a Gary nightclub. Playing at clubs gave the boys experience in front of live audiences. The performances also exposed them to a seedy world and adult entertainment—not the best places for children. But Joe continued to book such appearances, and Katherine, who was a devout Jehovah's Witness, tolerated these clubs because she also believed the experience could help her children become stars.

Motown Bends the Truth

Diana Ross is often credited with discovering the Jackson 5, but the story is a marketing message developed by the Motown recording label. The story claimed that Diana Ross, a big star in her own right, first saw the boys and brought them to the attention of Motown's Berry Gordy. Motown also told the public that the boys were two years younger than they really were, letting people believe that Michael was eight years old when he was actually ten. Although Ross did become a mentor to the boys—particularly Michael—fellow Motown recording artist Gladys Knight first introduced Motown executives to the band.

SUCCESS

These early Jackson 5 shows did help the family succeed. The boys won the amateur talent show at the Regal Theater in Chicago for three consecutive weeks in 1967. Following their successive wins, they opened for Gladys Knight and the Pips when the band performed at the theater. Knight, who was impressed with their performance during rehearsals, arranged for some Motown executives to hear the boys play that night.

▲ GLADYS KNIGHT AND THE PIPS HELPED LAUNCH THE JACKSON 5'S CAREER. THE BROTHERS WERE THE OPENING ACT FOR THE GROUP.

Opening for Gladys Knight and the Pips was the first of several opening engagements. The Jackson 5 opened for other big-name performers throughout that year, including the O'Jays, Jackie Wilson, the Temptations, and James Brown. Michael would stand offstage and watch the performers. He took in all he could to learn from these stars.

The Jackson 5 also took home another big prize in 1967. On August 13, the young band competed in—and won—the amateur night competition at the famed Apollo Theater in New York City. The Harlem venue had been a major spot for black talent since the 1930s. The boys' performance earned them a standing ovation, which was high praise from the tough crowd.

The performance schedule was tougher on the boys than their rehearsal schedule had been. The Jackson boys were often out past midnight, but they still had to be in school in the morning. Joe and Katherine also made sure their sons kept up with their homework and had passing grades in their classes.

ON THE RADIO

Music industry executives were taking notice as the boys were touring and winning talent shows. One such executive was Gordy Keith, owner of Steeltown Records in Gary. He signed the Jackson 5 to a contract and had the band record its first single, "Big Boy," in 1968. It was the first

Jackson 5 song ever played on the radio.

In the summer of 1968, Motown executives also took notice. They did not show much interest after the Jacksons' performance in 1967, when the boys opened for Gladys Knight and the Pips at the Regal Theater, but they were interested now. At this time, Jackie was 17, Tito was 14, Jermaine was 13, Marlon was 10, and Michael was only 9. The Jackson 5 had earned a chance to audition for Motown at the company's office in Detroit, Michigan, on July 23.

To make the audition, the boys had to miss their first scheduled television appearance, which was a planned spot on *The David Frost Show*. They were disappointed to miss their first chance to appear on national television, but they all understood—even young Michael—that auditioning for Motown was a big opportunity. If they succeeded in getting a contract, the siblings would have the chance to become stars.

The audition for Motown was very different from most of the performances that the Jackson 5 had given. The boys sang some of their usual

"I'm gonna make you the biggest thing in the world, and you're gonna be written about in history books."[2]
—*Motown Records CEO Berry Gordy to the Jackson 5 after signing the band to a recording contract*

songs, including the Motown tune "Who's Loving You?" The brothers did their best, but their audience of Motown workers did not applaud. They showed no sign of whether the boys had done well or whether Motown would offer them a contract. Instead, the Motown representatives just took notes. They then told the Jackson family that they would send Motown founder Berry Gordy a tape of the audition and get back to them with an answer.

The Jacksons did not have to wait long. Gordy reviewed the

Life Behind the Scenes

Motown liked to present the Jackson 5 as a wholesome family, but there was a lot of tension in the family. Joe Jackson was not only strict with his children, he was physically and emotionally abusive. In 1988, Michael wrote about his father:

We'd perform and he'd critique us. If you messed up, you got hit, sometimes with a belt, sometimes with a switch. My father was real strict with us—real strict. Marlon was the one who got in trouble all the time. On the other hand, I'd get beaten for things that happened mostly outside rehearsal. Dad would make me so mad and hurt that I'd try to get back at him and get beaten all the more.[3]

During the 2003 documentary *Living with Michael*, Jackson told journalist Martin Bashir that he was "terrified" of his father. Michael also said his father's presence caused him to faint and vomit from fear.[4]

Joe Jackson has claimed that he did not abuse his children. Referring to Michael, he said, "I whipped him with a switch and a belt. I never beat him. You beat someone with a stick."[5]

▲ BERRY GORDY SIGNED THE JACKSON BROTHERS TO A
RECORDING CONTRACT WITH MOTOWN RECORDS.

audition tape and offered the group a contract
within a few days.

THE JACKSON 5
ERA

 nce the Jacksons signed with Motown in 1968, the pressure was on to record hit songs. "Your first record will be a number one, your second record will be a number one, and so will your third record," Berry Gordy told the young performers and their father.[1]

The Motown music machine quickly went to work putting a team of producer-songwriters together. West Coast Creative Director Deke Richards, Freddie Perren, and Fonce Mizell were charged with turning the boys into hit-makers for

Motown. The three men called themselves the Corporation.

In 1969, the record company moved the musicians to Los Angeles, California, with their father. Just after their move, singer Diana Ross took the young group under her wing and helped get them even more publicity. She sent out invitations announcing a party at a trendy Beverly Hills disco—the Daisy— that would feature the Jackson 5. The show wowed the audience and won glowing reviews from the press. Michael and his brothers, who had stayed in hotels when they first arrived in California, later

Religion versus Stardom

Katherine Jackson, Michael's mother, became a Jehovah's Witness when Michael was five years old. Growing up, he often accompanied his mother to the Kingdom Hall of the Jehovah's Witnesses. He credited his mother for instilling him with a sense of gratefulness to God for the talent he had. "She taught me that my talent for singing and dancing was as much God's work as a beautiful sunset or a storm that left snow for children to play in," he said.[2]

Michael was baptized into the faith in 1981. But the strict religious beliefs of the Jehovah's Witnesses and the life of a music star were not always a good combination. Katherine often said she did not like the things that her children saw because they were stars, such as people smoking, drinking, and partying around her family. Michael also found it difficult to obey some of the religion's rules, such as not observing holidays and birthdays. Because he did not agree with many of the religion's beliefs, Michael withdrew from the Jehovah's Witnesses in 1987.

took turns staying at Ross's and Gordy's houses.

Not surprisingly, Michael missed his beloved mother and called her often. Katherine and the rest of the family had decided to stay in Gary until the Jackson 5's future in California was more secure. The family was not separated for long. By late 1969, they had moved to California.

"Michael was a born star. He was a classic example of understanding everything. I recognized that he had a depth that was so vast, it was just incredible. The first time I saw him, I saw this little kid as something real special."[3]
—Berry Gordy, Motown Records founder

TOPPING THE CHARTS

While the entire Jackson family was settling in to life on the West Coast, the Corporation was searching for the right song to launch the Jackson 5. Richards, Perren, and Mizell had a song called "I Want to Be Free" that was intended for Gladys Knight and the Pips, but they reworked it into "I Want You Back" for the Jackson 5. Released in November 1969, it became the Jackson 5's first Number 1 song. It was followed by a string of other Number 1 singles: "ABC," "The Love You Save," and "I'll Be There."

The Jackson 5's debut album, *Diana Ross Presents the Jackson 5*, was released in December 1969 and reached the top of the album charts.

▲ THE JACKSON 5'S FIRST ALBUM

NEW STARS

The Jackson brothers were stars. They performed on national television shows, including *The Ed Sullivan Show*, *The Flip Wilson Show*, *The Tonight Show*, *American Bandstand*, and *Soul Train*. The boys dressed in colorful clothes that were chosen to create a specific look. The brothers moved to well-rehearsed, carefully choreographed dance steps for each of their appearances. They toured nationally and internationally throughout the 1970s. Their shows drew tens of thousands of clamoring fans.

But the success and fame came at a price. Michael and his siblings had tried to attend classes at public and private schools in California, but it was impossible due to their schedules and the fans who would mob them. Instead, they learned from Rose Fine, a tutor who taught the boys between recording sessions, on concert tours, and while they traveled for television appearances. Michael, like his brothers, also had no time to play with children his own age. As a result, he often felt lonely and isolated. Later, as an adult, he wrote of his experience at that time and how he wanted to be like other children:

> There was a park across the street from the Motown studio, and I can remember looking

The Jackson 5 Animated

Watching Saturday morning cartoons has been a tradition for children over the years. Michael Jackson enjoyed weekend shows, but unlike other children, he watched himself as an animated character. *The Jackson 5ive* ran for two seasons from 1971 to 1973. The program's theme song was the group's hit single "ABC." Michael said of the experience, "I loved being a cartoon. It was so much fun to get up on Saturday mornings to watch cartoons and look forward to seeing ourselves on the screen. It was like a fantasy come true for all of us."[4]

at those kids playing games. I'd just stare at them in wonder—I couldn't imagine such freedom, such a carefree life—and wish more than anything that I had that kind of freedom, that I could walk away and be like them.[5]

Michael was shy as a boy and a teenager; life in the spotlight was often frightening to him. "Being mobbed by near hysterical girls was one of the most terrifying experiences for me in those days," he said.[6]

Despite the chaos that surrounded the brothers, the Jackson 5 continued to turn out hits during the 1970s. But the family's relationship with Motown soon grew strained. The brothers, supported by Joe, wanted to produce and record their own music and create their own unique sound. Motown wanted to stay with the formula of hits that had worked for the band.

In 1976, frustrated with the arrangements at Motown, Joe negotiated a deal for his sons with Epic Records, which

Motown Grooms the Boys for Success

Motown guided more than the musical careers of Michael Jackson and his brothers. The company groomed and carefully crafted an image of a tight-knit family that all Americans could admire. Much of this work fell to Motown employee Suzanne de Passe, who became a manager for the Jackson 5. She helped choose their clothes, taught them manners, worked with them on proper grammar, and showed them how to handle questions from fans and journalists. "Motown always told us what to say in interviews back then," Michael said.[7]

▲ THE JACKSON 5 PERFORMED ON *THE FLIP WILSON SHOW* IN 1971.

was then part of CBS Records. The contract allowed for the Jacksons to record songs they had written. It significantly boosted their royalty rate, which was the money they received for each album sold. The contract also gave the brothers the opportunity to record solo albums.

Michael, who was developing a sense of the business side of the music industry, was impressed. "This is one incredible record deal.

My father has done an amazing job for us," Michael said.[8]

But Michael also found the split with Motown painful. He admired Berry Gordy and wanted to be loyal to him. He felt sad that his brother Jermaine, who had married Gordy's daughter, decided to stay with Motown and not move to Epic. But Michael also knew that artists needed control over their work and fair compensation for it. He was concerned that if the Jacksons remained at Motown they would have to perform "oldies," songs that were once popular but are not so anymore. He realized that the move to Epic was for the best.

The switch in record labels brought some notable changes for the Jacksons. Because Motown claimed legal rights to the name "Jackson 5," the group became simply the Jacksons. Randy replaced Jermaine in the lineup. The brothers' music started to move forward with songs

Some Jackson 5 Hits

Some of the music highlights for the Jackson 5 during the 1970s:

- 1970: *ABC*, the Jackson 5's second album, is released, followed by the *Third Album* and *The Jackson 5 Christmas Album*.
- 1974: The brothers star in their own show at the MGM Grand Hotel in Las Vegas, Nevada. Siblings Janet, LaToya, and Randy also appear onstage.
- 1974: The song "Dancing Machine," from the album of the same name, hits Number 2 on the Billboard pop chart.
- 1978: The Jacksons release *Destiny*, their first self-produced album, featuring songs the group wrote.

▲ MICHAEL JACKSON, *BACK RIGHT,* WITH HIS BROTHERS, MARLON, TITO, RANDY, AND JACKIE

that had more of a dance beat, which provided a glimpse of what was ahead for Michael as a solo artist.

5

GOING SOLO

ichael Jackson clearly shined bright as the lead singer for the Jackson 5, but his first several solo albums failed to garner much attention or praise. He released four albums in five years—all while only a teenager. His first, *Got To Be There*, was released in November 1971 on the Motown label. He released his second album, *Ben*, the following year. These albums did moderately well. His next two albums did only a fraction as well. *Music and Me* came out in 1973, and *Forever Michael* came out in 1975.

▶ MICHAEL JACKSON EXPERIENCED SUCCESS WITH HIS BROTHERS, BUT HE WANTED A SOLO CAREER.

Unlike his experience with the family band, Jackson had only one song from his four solo albums that became popular. "Ben" was the title song from his second album. It was the theme song for a horror movie about a sick boy who was befriended by a telepathic rat. The song made it to the top position on the Billboard Hot 100. It also received a Golden Globe Award and an Oscar nomination.

Jackson's early attempts at a solo career did not have much success. This left many people doubtful that the young singer could break free from his brothers and become a performer in his own right. But Jackson would prove the doubters wrong.

A New Partnership

After the success of the Jacksons' 1978 release, *Destiny*, Jackson decided to seriously pursue a solo career. He wanted to sing on his own and establish his own musical style. But Jackson's father and brothers were not happy about Jackson's ambitions.

High-profile Dating

Although Michael Jackson experienced great loneliness, he met and socialized with many other famous people while growing up. He partied with other celebrities at New York City's famous Studio 54 while he was in New York City filming *The Wiz*. He also dated some high-profile women during the late 1970s and early 1980s. He dated Tatum O'Neal, who had also grown up in the spotlight because she had been an actress since she was a child. Later, he dated Brooke Shields, another performer who had started acting in films as a child.

▲ MICHAEL JACKSON, *RIGHT*, MADE HIS FILM DEBUT AS THE SCARECROW IN *THE WIZ*.

The five siblings had always performed as a group, and they knew that Jackson's talent had been a key factor in their success. They thought that the group would be less successful without him and discouraged Jackson from pursuing creative opportunities that were offered to him. Jackson had been asked to appear in *The Wiz*, a remake of *The Wizard of Oz*. This version was set in 1970s Harlem in New York City instead of a farm in Kansas.

But Jackson had made up his mind. He wanted to break away from his family, so he started to make decisions to put him on the path to a solo career. For example, Jackson took the role of the Scarecrow in *The Wiz* despite his family's desire that he turn down the offer. The movie featured an all-black cast and introduced the story to a new audience with new songs, such as "Ease On Down The Road." The movie did not do well at the box office and was

The Wiz

Michael Jackson had appeared on television shows dozens of times as a child. In 1977, he had an opportunity to appear in a movie. Jackson earned the role of the Scarecrow in the film version of *The Wiz*, an adaptation of the classic *Wizard of Oz* set in modern-day Harlem and featuring an African-American cast.

The movie starred Jackson's close friend and mentor Diana Ross, who had encouraged him to audition for the part. Rob Cohen, head of Motown Productions, commented on casting Jackson, "I was always impressed by Michael Jackson. He struck me as being so polished, yet still pure. Plus he could sing . . . and this was a musical."[1]

The opportunity gave Jackson a chance to stretch his performing skills in new ways, and he found the experience both stressful and exciting. The experience also gave Jackson, who temporarily relocated to New York with sister LaToya for the filming, a taste of living away from the Jackson home in California for the first time.

widely criticized. But Jackson enjoyed making the film and wanted to do more acting following this experience.

As he moved ahead with his solo plans, Jackson hired his own record producer, Quincy Jones. Jackson had met Jones while they were both working on *The Wiz*. Although Jones was a well-established figure in the music business, he was better known for his work with jazz musicians and R & B acts. When Jackson decided to look for his own producer, he did not initially consider Jones. Rather, the singer called Jones to ask for advice and recommendations for a producer for his solo album. After talking with Jackson about his ideas for the album, Jones said he would like to be Jackson's producer. Jackson agreed.

Together, Jackson and Jones considered what kind of sound they wanted for Jackson's

Paul McCartney's Contributions

Years before Michael Jackson started recording *Off The Wall*, superstar Paul McCartney wrote a song called "Girlfriend" for Jackson to record. Quincy Jones suggested using it for *Off The Wall*. This would be the first of three collaborations with McCartney, a member of the legendary group the Beatles. The two singers went on to record "The Girl Is Mine" for Jackson's 1982 release, *Thriller*, and "Say, Say, Say" for McCartney's 1983 *Pipes of Peace*. Their friendship later became strained when Jackson bought the publishing rights to the Beatles' song catalogue in 1984 as part of his $47.5 million purchase of the ATV Music Publishing Company.

solo project. Jackson knew he did not want something that sounded similar to *Destiny*. He knew he wanted something that was different from anything he had done with his brothers. "That's why I wanted to hire an outside producer who wouldn't come to this project with any preconceived notions about how it should sound," Jackson said.[2] He also wanted someone to help him select songs written by others to accompany the ones he had penned himself.

OFF THE WALL

Jackson and Jones started working on the album *Off The Wall* in late 1978 and continued into the spring of 1979. Jones guided Jackson in his musical growth, teaching him new musical techniques to stretch his vocal range and broaden his selection of musical themes.

Although the pair wanted a more mature sound for Jackson's solo album, Jones remembered the singer as being painfully shy. Jones described working with Jackson, saying, "He was so shy, he'd sit down and sing behind the couch with his

"Making *Off The Wall* was one of the most difficult periods of my life, despite the eventual success it enjoyed. I had very few close friends at the time and felt very isolated. I was so lonely that I used to walk through my neighborhood hoping I'd run into somebody I could talk to and perhaps become friends with."[3]

—Michael Jackson

▲ QUINCY JONES PRODUCED MICHAEL JACKSON'S
OFF THE WALL ALBUM.

back to me, while I sat there with my hands over
my eyes with the lights off."[4]

The singer and the producer sorted
through all the possible selections for songs.
They narrowed down the list of compositions
that would make up *Off The Wall*. Three of
Jackson's songs—"Don't Stop 'Til You Get
Enough," "Working Day and Night," and "Get
on the Floor," which was cowritten with Louis

Johnson—made the cut. Those funky, dance-inspired cuts were mixed with ballads and pop tunes and put Jackson on the map as a solo artist.

Jackson's hard work on *Off The Wall* impressed Jones, who predicted that the young performer was "going to be *the* star of the eighties and nineties."[5] The album was released during the summer of 1979, just weeks before Jackson's twenty-first birthday. It put him on the path to becoming a solo superstar.

The album produced two Number 1 hits on the Billboard Hot 100: "Don't Stop 'Til You Get Enough" and "Rock With You." The songs "Off The Wall" and "She's Out of My Life" both peaked at the Number 10 spot. Album sales exceeded 20 million copies worldwide, peaking in the United States at Number 3 and staying on the Billboard Top 20 for 48 weeks. Jackson was the first solo artist to have four Top 10 singles from one album.

Given the success of his album, Jackson was disappointed when the Grammy nominations for 1979 were announced.

The *Off The Wall* Playlist

Michael Jackson's album *Off The Wall* has ten songs:
- "Don't Stop 'Till You Get Enough"
- "Rock With You"
- "Working Day and Night"
- "Get On the Floor"
- "Off The Wall"
- "Girlfriend"
- "She's Out Of My Life"
- "I Can't Help It"
- "It's The Falling In Love"
- "Burn This Disco Out"

▲ MICHAEL JACKSON'S *OFF THE WALL* GARNERED ONE GRAMMY NOMINATION, BUT MORE NOMINATIONS—AND WINS—WERE IN HIS FUTURE.

Jackson had received only one nomination: Best R & B Vocal Performance, Male. He thought he deserved more nominations because *Off The Wall* was such a big hit. Jackson did not hide his disappointment. He won the Grammy, but he promised that so few nominations would not happen again, saying, "You watch. The next album I do, you watch. I'll show them."[6]

6

THRILLER

ichael Jackson had one clear goal since he was a child: to have the best-selling album ever. "Ever since I was a little boy, I had dreamed of creating the biggest-selling record of all time," Jackson said.[1] He made no secret that he wanted the solo album that followed his successful *Off The Wall* to fulfill that dream.

Making that happen, however, was no easy feat. Jackson and Quincy Jones teamed again to make this album. They had the challenging task of finding the right mix of songs that could send

▶ MICHAEL JACKSON'S *THRILLER* BECAME A RECORD-BREAKING ALBUM.

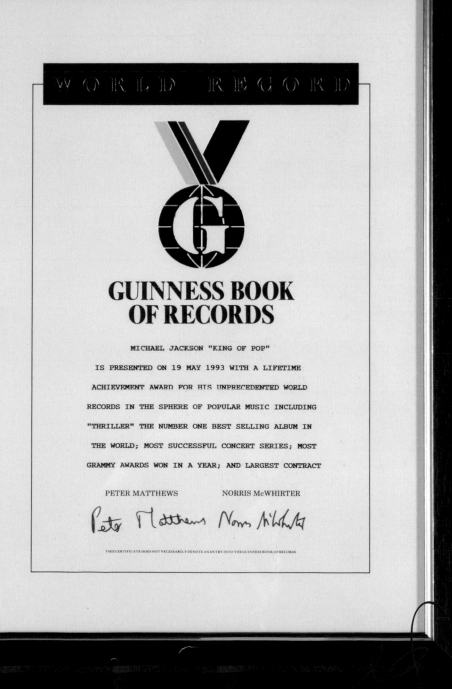

WORLD RECORD

GUINNESS BOOK OF RECORDS

MICHAEL JACKSON "KING OF POP"

IS PRESENTED ON 19 MAY 1993 WITH A LIFETIME

ACHIEVEMENT AWARD FOR HIS UNPRECEDENTED WORLD

RECORDS IN THE SPHERE OF POPULAR MUSIC INCLUDING

"THRILLER" THE NUMBER ONE BEST SELLING ALBUM IN

THE WORLD; MOST SUCCESSFUL CONCERT SERIES; MOST

GRAMMY AWARDS WON IN A YEAR; AND LARGEST CONTRACT

PETER MATTHEWS   NORRIS McWHIRTER

THIS CERTIFICATE DOES NOT NECESSARILY DENOTE AN ENTRY INTO THE GUINNESS BOOK OF RECORDS

Jackson's career soaring to new heights. They sorted through hundreds of songs and finally settled on nine.

WORTH THE WAIT

The two men spent the second half of 1982 in the studio recording the tracks for what would become *Thriller*. As the production team worked on mixing the tracks for the album, it became clear that *Thriller* would not match the success of *Off The Wall*. CBS Records had pressured Jackson's team to finish its work quickly. As a result, Jackson felt the final mix was rushed and not done correctly. Jackson was devastated when he first heard the album, but he was not defeated. He told CBS and his own production team to slow down and mix the songs again until they had it right. *Thriller* was finally released on December 1, 1982.

Music critics were impressed with the end result. *Rolling Stone* magazine's Christopher Connelly wrote about "the surprising substance of 'Thriller'. . . . Jackson has cooked up a zesty LP whose uptempo workouts

The *Thriller* Playlist

Michael Jackson's *Thriller* album had nine songs:
- "Wanna Be Startin' Something"
- "Baby Be Mine"
- "The Girl Is Mine"
- "Thriller"
- "Beat It"
- "Billie Jean"
- "Human Nature"
- "P.Y.T. (Pretty Young Thing)"
- "The Lady In My Life"

don't obscure its harrowing, dark messages."[2]

As Jackson predicted, *Thriller* became a huge success. It sold 30 million copies in two years. Seven of its nine singles became Top 10 hits, including "Beat It," "Billie Jean," and the title song, "Thriller." The album stayed at the Number 1 spot on the Billboard charts for 37 weeks. It eventually sold more than 50 million copies worldwide, becoming the biggest-selling record of all time, according to the *Guinness Book of World Records*.

Bringing E.T. to Life

Michael Jackson and Quincy Jones collaborated on another project about the time they were making the *Thriller* album. The pair also made the album *E.T.: The Extra Terrestrial*. Moviemaker Steven Spielberg had directed the 1982 movie by the same name, which is the story of a lonely boy who becomes friends with an alien left behind while visiting Earth. Spielberg hired Jones to produce the storybook *E.T.* album, and they asked Jackson to narrate the story. The collaboration earned Jackson and Jones a Grammy in 1983 for Best Recording for Children.

BREAKING BARRIERS, SETTING RECORDS

Jackson's music alone did not create the phenomenon of *Thriller*. Jackson's music videos, like his dazzling performance at the 1983 Motown special, captivated viewers and won new listeners. At that time, many singers made videos that only showed them singing and playing their instruments during concerts. Jackson wanted to create short films. "I wanted to make the best short music movies we could make," he explained.[3]

Jackson's music videos broke down racial barriers at MTV, which in 1983 was only 16 months old. Although executives from CBS Records and MTV told different stories about what happened, CBS said MTV would not play Jackson's "Billie Jean" video. At that time, MTV did not play many songs by black musicians. CBS told MTV that the record company would not do business with it any more if "Billie Jean" did not make it on the air. MTV soon started playing the "Billie Jean" video, which opened the door for other

Putting Music to Work

Michael Jackson put his star power to charitable use in early 1985, when he teamed with Lionel Richie to write and record "We Are the World" to raise money for and awareness of famine relief in Africa.

Jackson and Richie recruited 45 artists to join the January 28, 1985, recording session at A&M Studios in Hollywood following the American Music Awards held earlier that evening. The musicians who participated were some of the biggest stars at that time, including Billy Joel, Bruce Springsteen, and Stevie Wonder. Several of Jackson's siblings also took part. Legendary performers Ray Charles and Bob Dylan also helped out. Quincy Jones produced the record and directed the singers.

"We Are the World" was released on March 7, 1985. It became the fastest-selling single ever. It topped charts around the world for weeks, raising more than $6.5 million in its first two months—and tens of millions of dollars over the years—to benefit the relief organization USA for Africa.

▲ ICONIC ARTIST ANDY WARHOL PAINTED THIS PORTRAIT
OF MICHAEL JACKSON IN HONOR OF *THRILLER*'S SUCCESS.

black artists to get airtime on the cable station.
"That was the video that broke the color barrier,"
Jackson comanager Ron Weisner said.[4]

With its creative lighting and camera work,
"Billie Jean" became a smash. "Beat It," which
featured famous rock band guitarist Eddie Van
Halen and actual gang members dancing behind
Jackson, was just as popular.

The video for the song "Thriller" raised the standards for video-making even higher. "Thriller" cost more than $500,000 to make. Videos by other musicians at that time cost a fraction of that amount, just tens of thousands of dollars. Unlike most videos that were only a few minutes long, "Thriller" was a 14-minute movie featuring dancing zombies. It debuted on MTV in December 1983 and became a pop sensation. But not all who saw the video approved of it. Some people criticized the video for its monsters and portrayal of supernatural events. Leaders of the Jehovah's Witnesses told Jackson that they did not like the video's content. Jackson responded by putting in a disclaimer at the start of the video that the film does not mean that he believes in the occult. Despite the controversy around the "Thriller" video, a documentary called *Making Michael Jackson's "Thriller"* became a hit, too. "Michael Jackson defined the video as an art form," Rob Sheffield wrote of the performer in *Rolling Stone* magazine.[5]

Family Pressures

As the family patriarch, Joe Jackson had stressed family prosperity over individual success. And he did so again in 1983 when he pressured Michael to join his brothers in a reunion concert tour that would take them around the world. Michael was against the idea. "I didn't want to go on the Victory tour and I fought against it. I felt the wisest thing for me would be not to do the tour, but my brothers wanted to do it and I did it for them," he said.[6]

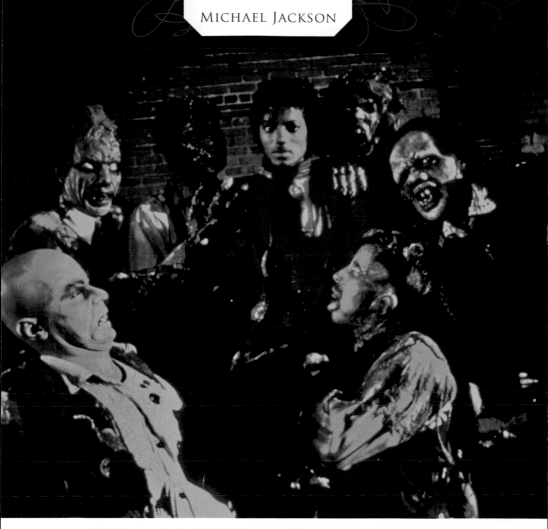

▲ MICHAEL JACKSON'S "THRILLER" VIDEO CHANGED THE
WORLD OF MUSIC VIDEOS.

Jackson's popularity was soaring, but it had
exploded following the May 1983 Motown
anniversary special in which Jackson wowed the
crowd with his music and his moves. "Everyone
forgets that all those Motown giants and legends
were on the show. The next day all anyone was
talking about was Michael," Weisner said.[7]

Jackson won an unprecedented eight Grammys for *Thriller*, including Best Album, Best Pop Vocal Performance for a Male, and Best Video Album. He had achieved great success with *Thriller* and made tens of millions of dollars, but Jackson did not slow down. While *Thriller* was climbing the charts and winning awards, he was talking about writing his autobiography with Jacqueline Kennedy Onassis, who was an editor for the publisher Doubleday.

Michael Jackson seemed to have everything he had wished for, but he was not necessarily happy. He was feeling pressure from his brothers to tour with them, but he did not want to go. He felt he had worked hard to become successful as a solo artist. He did not want the public to see him once again as only part of the Jacksons. But his brothers did not have the same success in attempts at their own solo careers—they needed the money that sales from a tour would bring. They wanted their lead singer

Filming Gone Wrong

Michael Jackson and his brothers signed on to film two commercials in 1984 for the Pepsi-Cola Company, which was sponsoring their world tour. Although the job seemed simple enough—just sing and dance—there was an accident during the filming. On January 27, as Michael walked down a set of stairs with pyrotechnics going off, a spark set fire to his hair. He was rushed to the hospital. The accident left Jackson with third-degree burns on his head. This would ultimately change his life in ways that would not be made public until many years later.

▲ MICHAEL JACKSON, *CENTER*, CIRCA 1983

back, especially since he was now so popular.
In the end, Jackson agreed to participate in the
world tour for the sake of his family.

———•◆•———

7

A LIFE OF FAME

y the mid-1980s, Michael Jackson had spent nearly two decades—most of his young life—in the public eye. With multiple successes, he felt the pressure to deliver even more. So, he started working on the album that would follow his widely popular *Thriller*.

CHALLENGES OF FAME

Jackson tried to keep a low profile for nearly two years as he worked on his follow-up album. But Jackson was one of the most famous people

▸ MICHAEL JACKSON ATTRACTED ATTENTION WHEREVER HE WENT. HE HAD FANS WORLDWIDE.

in the world. For much of his life, he had to deal with fans, but his latest success was unlike any he had experienced before. Fans mobbed Jackson in public. He was unable to perform everyday activities such as shopping without being bothered. Being mobbed by fans was a frightening experience physically and emotionally. Fans could be difficult, too. Some would demand an autograph rather than ask for one. Some would say how much they loved him even though they did not know him.

In 1981, one teenager wrote dozens of letters to Jackson saying that she had given birth to his baby, though the two had never met. Jackson said in his autobiography that his song "Billie Jean" was not about the fan, but some people speculated that this fan at least in part inspired the lyrics. Jackson would deal with other unstable fans throughout his life.

Jackson's fame brought him in contact with a host of famous people, including world leaders. He had met Britain's Queen Elizabeth II when the Jackson 5 toured England in 1972. He met U.S. President Ronald

Jackson's Pets

Michael Jackson kept an interesting array of pets over the years, sometimes bringing them on tour or out in public. His collection of animals included Bubbles the Chimp, a boa constrictor named Muscles, and Jabar the Giraffe. He also had llamas, peacocks, and a variety of birds.

Reagan in May 1984, when the president gave him a special citation for letting the government use "Beat It" in commercials warning against driving drunk. Jackson had become friendly with several other high-profile celebrities, including actresses Elizabeth Taylor and Liza Minnelli, and was photographed at social events with them.

BAD

Quincy Jones worked with Jackson on his next album. *Bad* came out on October 1, 1987. A self-described perfectionist, Jackson said he wanted this album to be "as close to perfect as humanly possible."[1] Music critics said that *Bad* was actually quite good. "*Bad* is the work of a gifted singer-songwriter," Davitt Sigerson wrote in his October 1987 review for *Rolling Stone* magazine. He continued, "Comparisons with *Thriller* are unimportant, except this one: even without a milestone recording like 'Billie Jean,' *Bad* is a better record."[2]

Shut in Neverland

Throughout the 1990s and into the 2000s, Michael Jackson spent an increasing amount of time shut behind the walls of Neverland, the ranch he purchased in 1988 for millions of dollars. Reports of how much Jackson paid for the property vary from less than $20 million to nearly $30 million. Jackson had lived there more than 15 years, transforming the ranch into a fantasy land with carnival rides and zoo animals. In addition to being his own personal refuge, Jackson used the property to entertain less-fortunate and sick children.

▲ MICHAEL JACKSON MET CELEBRITIES AND WORLD LEADERS, INCLUDING ENGLAND'S PRINCE CHARLES AND PRINCESS DIANA.

The album debuted at the top spot on the Billboard Album Chart. Five of the tracks became Number 1 singles. *Bad* sold more than 25 million copies. Jackson followed the release of *Bad* with a world tour from September 1987 through January 1989. The Bad World Tour was his first solo concert series.

A MESSAGE FROM JACKSON

Over the years, many of Jackson's songs, including those on *Bad*, have contained personal messages. "Man in The Mirror" talks about Jackson's belief that people who want to make things better have to start by making themselves better. In his song "Leave Me Alone," which was only on the compact disc version of *Bad* and not the vinyl album version, Jackson told people to stay away from him. "What I'm really saying to people who are bothering me is: '*Leave me alone*,'" Jackson said.[3] Jackson said that he found it difficult to be famous:

> *The price of fame can be a heavy one. . . . Consider that you really have no privacy. You can't really do anything unless special arrangements are made. The media prints whatever you say. They report whatever you do.*[4]

Despite the message of "Leave Me Alone," Jackson's life had become even less private

Telling His Own Story

In 1988, Michael Jackson released his autobiography, *Moonwalk*. He was 29 years old. The book chronicles Jackson's life from his earliest memories in Gary, Indiana, through the release of his album *Bad* in 1987. "*Moonwalk* provides a startling glimpse of the artist at work and the artist in reflection," editor Jacqueline Kennedy Onassis wrote at the beginning of the book.[5]

following the release and success of *Thriller*. Many newspaper stories criticized his childlike demeanor and his decisions to pal around with children. Stories criticized him for his sometimes odd behaviors. For example, Jackson sometimes wore a surgical mask in public. Journalists also started to speculate that Jackson was having plastic surgery to change how he looked. Many people began criticizing his dance moves, too, because he had started to grab his crotch while performing.

KING OF POP

Still, Jackson had great successes and countless fans. His achievements earned him the nickname the "King of Pop," but some in the media had dubbed him

---

Jackson's Ever-changing Appearance

Michael Jackson's face changed a lot throughout his life, and it was not only a result of aging. Jackson said that he felt awkward about how he looked and shy during his teens because he had acne. Some family members also teased him about his nose, saying it was too big.

Jackson decided to have surgery to change his appearance. He admitted that he had a few surgeries to make his nose smaller and to add a cleft to his chin. He also said his face became thinner because he stopped eating meat and became a vegetarian. He said his skin became lighter because he had a skin disorder called vitiligo.

However, many people suspect that he had many more surgeries than he admitted. Some news stories said that doctors might have changed the shape of his eyes, lips, and cheeks—even the bones in his face were possibly reconstructed. Other reports said Jackson might have used a chemical to lighten the color of his skin.

▲ MICHAEL JACKSON TOURED THE WORLD PERFORMING CONCERTS TO PROMOTE HIS ALBUMS.

"Wacko Jacko" for his odd behavior. To escape from such name-calling, Jackson developed his own refuge at Neverland, the estate and carnival-like grounds he created on more than 2,500 acres (1,012 ha) in Los Olivos, California.

Jackson continued to produce popular music. He followed *Bad* with the 1991 release of the album *Dangerous*, which sold approximately 27 million copies. The album produced four Top 10 singles in the United States, including the Number 1 song "Black Or White."

TARNISHED IMAGE

Even with all the attention that Jackson was receiving as a singer, his music was not getting as much attention as his private life. In early 1993, Jackson was in trouble after a 13-year-old boy said the entertainer had touched him inappropriately. Police in California investigated the boy's story, but they did not arrest Jackson. The boy's family filed a civil lawsuit against Jackson, but Jackson signed an agreement with the boy's family in 1994. News reports said Jackson agreed to pay the boy as much as $20 million.

Jackson said he did not do anything wrong. His attorney said Jackson was not guilty. He argued, "He is an innocent man who does not intend to have his career and his life destroyed by rumor and innuendo."[6]

Although Jackson said he was innocent, the boy's story had damaged Jackson's image around the world. Following the settlement with the boy's family, Jackson ended his tour for *Dangerous*, canceling the remainder of the shows

▲ MICHAEL JACKSON PRESENTED HIS MOTHER, KATHERINE, WITH THE FIRST COPY OF HIS AUTOBIOGRAPHY, *MOONWALK*.

that had been scheduled. He explained that he had become addicted to painkillers as a result of the charges that had been made against him. Jackson went on to say that he was entering a special program to get treatment for his addiction to drugs.

8

MARRIAGE, FAMILY, AND CONTROVERSY

ichael Jackson's life throughout the 1990s was turbulent. He continued to make new music, but he became more famous for his unpredictable and often controversial behavior than his songs. Jackson seemed to prefer hanging out with children rather than adults. He had taken children as guests to public events, and he traveled with them. They also spent time at his home. In addition, Jackson had a lifelong affection for a childhood pastime: watching cartoons. But his frequent association and

▶ MICHAEL JACKSON AND LISA MARIE PRESLEY WERE MARRIED BRIEFLY.

friendships with children created controversy. The public thought such behavior was odd for a grown man.

Spending time with children was not Jackson's only shocking behavior. On May 26, 1994, Jackson married Lisa Marie Presley, the daughter of rock-and-roll legend Elvis Presley. Jackson and Lisa Marie Presley had first met in 1974 backstage at a Jackson 5 concert. The two celebrities became friends in the late 1980s. Although they had been friends for six years before their wedding in the Dominican Republic, many suspected Jackson had married her as a way to repair his damaged reputation. Their public appearances seemed phony. The couple shared an awkward kiss at the MTV Video Music Awards in September 1994. And they did not seem very happy together when Presley appeared in Jackson's romantic 1995 video for "You Are Not Alone." Their marriage lasted less than two years. The couple filed for divorce in January 1996.

"Our relationship was not 'a sham' as is being reported in the press. It was an unusual relationship yes, where two unusual people who did not live or know a 'Normal life' found a connection, perhaps with some suspect timing on his part. Nonetheless, I do believe he loved me as much as he could love anyone and I loved him very much."[1]
—Lisa Marie Presley, posted on her MySpace blog on June 26, 2009

But Jackson remarried quickly. On November 15, 1996, he married Deborah "Debbie" Rowe, a nursing assistant who worked in his dermatologist's office. The two had been friends for a few years. They married while Jackson was on tour in Australia. Rowe gave birth to a son, Prince Michael Joseph Jackson, on February 13, 1997. Daughter Paris Michael Katherine Jackson was born on April 3, 1998. But this marriage also lasted less than two years. The couple divorced in October 1999. Rowe received a multimillion-dollar settlement, and Jackson was given custody of the two children.

Jackson added a third child to his family, a son born in 2002, called Prince Michael Joseph Jackson II, or Blanket. Jackson never publicly identified the boy's mother.

STILL MAKING MUSIC

Jackson did not have as many hits during the 1990s, but he did not ignore his music career. He spent months on the Dangerous World Tour, which ran from June 1992 through November 1993 and took him around the world.

Criticized as a Parent

Even as a parent, Michael Jackson could not escape controversy. He was criticized for holding his infant son Blanket over a hotel balcony in Berlin in 2002. He was also criticized for having his children appear in public wearing masks.

In 1995, Jackson released *HIStory: Past, Present, and Future.* As the name suggests, the two-CD set had some Jackson hits, including "Billie Jean," "Bad," and "Black Or White." *HIStory* also had new songs, such as "They Don't Care About Us."

Jackson's *HIStory* hit Number 1 on the album chart and gave him three Top 10 hit singles. The song "You Are Not Alone" became a Number 1 hit, and "Childhood" reached Number 5. The album featured "Scream," a duet with younger sister Janet. The song also reached Number 5 on the Billboard charts. But "They Don't Care About Us" failed to break 30 on the Billboard single charts, making it a disappointing peak for the megastar.

Following the release of that album, Jackson once again set out on tour. The HIStory World Tour took him around the world from September 1996 to October 1997.

Jackson released two more albums. *Blood on the Dance Floor*, which featured a number of existing songs that were remixed for a new dance-

"Scream"

Michael Jackson made another music video milestone when he released "Scream" in 1995. The song and video featured Jackson singing with his sister Janet. It cost $7 million for the outer space-themed visuals and was the most expensive video ever made. It won a Grammy for Best Music Video, Short Form.

▲ MICHAEL JACKSON CAUSED A LARGE CONTROVERSY
WHEN HE HELD HIS BABY OVER THE EDGE OF A BALCONY
IN 2002.

oriented sound, was released in 1997. *Invincible* followed in 2001 and gave Jackson one final Top 10 hit, "You Rock My World." Neither album matched any of his earlier work in sales or critical acclaim.

MORE TROUBLE

Rather than achieving great success, Jackson found himself in more trouble. Another boy

▲ MICHAEL JACKSON RECEIVED CONSIDERABLE ATTENTION AND CRITICISM FOR HIS CHANGE IN APPEARANCE OVER THE YEARS.

accused him of inappropriate contact. This time, police charged Jackson with a crime and arrested him in late 2003 on assault charges. In 2005, Jackson went on trial where a jury heard the evidence. His former wife, Debbie Rowe, was one of his most important defenders. She said that Jackson was "a good father" and "great with kids."[2] On June 14, the jury determined Jackson was not guilty.

But the criminal charges and trial had an impact on Jackson. He decided not to return to Neverland, which the police had raided during their investigation. Jackson was also having trouble with his finances during this time and owed a lot of people money. To get away from his problems, Jackson spent much of the next few years living in Bahrain, a country located in the Middle East. "They didn't treat him right here. I know if I was him, I wouldn't come back," said Joe Jackson of his son.[3]

Michael Jackson kept a low profile for the next several years, making only brief formal appearances in public, such as his performance at the World Music Awards in 2006 to sing "We Are the World."

Eventually, Jackson decided to return to the music he loved. In early 2009, the singer

Final Performance

At a March 2009 press conference, Michael Jackson announced that he would be performing a number of concerts at London's O2 arena that summer. He told the cheering crowd, "This is it, when I say this is it, this is it. I'll be performing the songs my fans want to hear—this is it. This is really it. This is the final curtain call. I'll see you in July."[4]

announced that he would play 50 concerts at London's O2 arena. The shows were sold out the day tickets went on sale—millions of tickets were sold within hours. Despite the controversy that surrounded him during the previous 15 years, fans still wanted to see Jackson perform his music. But the concerts would never take place.

———— • ◆ • ————

Living with Michael

The 2003 documentary *Living with Michael* gave millions of people a rare and controversial look into Michael Jackson's private life and personal thoughts. British station ITV made the documentary. Journalist Martin Bashir followed Jackson around the world for months.

During that time, Jackson talked about sleeping in the same bed with children at Neverland ranch. Jackson was also filmed holding hands with the 13-year-old boy who accused him of inappropriately touching him. Jackson told Bashir that he thought holding hands was innocent and loving. But public reaction to the 90-minute documentary showed that many people did not share Jackson's views.

Bashir later joined the ABC network in the United States. On June 25, 2009, after Jackson's death, Bashir reflected on *Living with Michael* during a *Nightline* news show broadcast, stating:

It's worth remembering that he was probably, singly, the greatest dancer and musician the world has ever seen. . . . His lifestyle may have been unorthodox, [but] I don't believe it was criminal.[5]

KING OF POP
MICHAEL
JACKSON
THIS IS IT

▲ IN MARCH 2009, MICHAEL JACKSON ANNOUNCED A
50-CONCERT TOUR IN LONDON, ENGLAND.

9

DEAD AT 50

he news traveled at lightning speed: Michael Jackson, a worldwide star, was dead at age 50. The story broke in the early afternoon, Pacific time, on June 25, 2009. An emergency 911 call had come from Jackson's Los Angeles home—a caller stated Jackson was not breathing. The Los Angeles County Coroner's office soon confirmed that he had died, apparently of a heart attack.

Like his life, Jackson's death was surrounded by controversy. Police immediately started to gather information. Rescue workers and Jackson

▶ JERMAINE JACKSON, WEARING A SINGLE GLOVE, PERFORMED AT HIS BROTHER'S MEMORIAL SERVICE.

family members questioned how someone so young could die so unexpectedly. But even as police and journalists wondered about the cause of his death, fans around the world put aside their questions with public displays of mourning for Jackson, the "King of Pop."

THE MEMORIAL SERVICE

A July 7, 2009, memorial service brought 25,000 people—with approximately 1,000 of them gathered outside watching a simulcast—to the Staples Center arena in Los Angeles, California, to say good-bye to Jackson. Brothers Jackie, Jermaine, Randy, and Tito carried Michael's rose-covered casket onto the stage. They all wore gold ties and a single sequined white glove, a clear tribute to the brother who had made wearing a single sparkling glove his signature look in the 1980s.

Jackson family members, longtime friends, and fellow musicians paid tribute to Jackson during the service, which was broadcast worldwide. Tributes included Jermaine singing

Inducted Twice

Michael Jackson was inducted twice into the Rock and Roll Hall of Fame and Museum in Cleveland, Ohio. The first time was in 1997, when he and his brothers Jackie, Jermaine, Marlon, and Tito received the honor as the Jackson 5. The second induction was in 2001. This time, Jackson was honored for his solo contributions to the music industry. The museum displays a permanent exhibition dedicated to Michael Jackson in the Legends of Rock exhibit.

▲ FANS WORLDWIDE CREATED MAKESHIFT MEMORIALS, INCLUDING THIS ONE OUTSIDE THE APOLLO THEATER IN NEW YORK CITY.

Charlie Chaplin's "Smile" and longtime friend Brooke Shields saying a final farewell. The day's performers paid a final tribute, singing a rendition of "We Are the World," the song Jackson cowrote with Lionel Richie in 1985. More than 30 million people in the United States watched the service on television.

CONTROVERSIAL TO THE END

Tears and tributes promptly gave way to controversy and court hearings. Investigators focused on Jackson's alleged abuse of prescription drugs. News reports said he was addicted to prescription drugs, including painkillers he had started taking after being severely burned in 1984. Investigators were also looking at the role Jackson's doctors played in this case and whether any should face criminal charges.

Courts addressed the fate of Michael's three children, 12-year-old Prince, 11-year-old Paris, and 7-year-old Blanket. In August 2009, a judge granted permanent custody to Jackson's mother, Katherine. But questions remained about what would happen to Jackson's estate and exactly how much it was worth. Estimates put Jackson's assets at hundreds of millions of dollars and possibly into the billions—but he owed hundreds of millions of dollars, too.

Jackson's death became the focus of much media attention, just as his life

A Fourth Child?

In the weeks following his death, speculation grew that Michael Jackson had a fourth child. Joe Jackson, Michael's father, claimed that Omer Bhatti, a 25-year-old dancer and rapper from Norway, was Jackson's oldest child. Others close to Jackson, however, say he is not. Jackson had never acknowledged a fourth child, but Bhatti did attend Jackson's televised memorial service, sitting with Jackson's children and siblings in the front row.

▲ TWO OF MICHAEL JACKSON'S CHILDREN, PARIS AND PRINCE MICHAEL I, ATTEND THEIR FATHER'S MEMORIAL SERVICE.

had been. News reports talked about his accomplishments in life and what he left behind. His will became a much-discussed document. In it, he left his fortune to his mother, his children, and several children's charities. According to news reports, Jackson left nothing to his brothers or his father.

Even in death, Jackson could not escape disputes and controversy. Some family members sought to have Jackson buried at his Neverland ranch, but he was eventually buried in a mausoleum at Forest Lawn Cemetery, a famed final resting place in Hollywood Hills, California. In the months following Jackson's death, news stories reported that he might not have been the biological father to some or all of his three children.

HIS LEGACY

Jackson's career peaked in the mid-1980s with the release of his best-selling *Thriller* and its follow-up

Berry Gordy's Statement

Following the death of Michael Jackson on June 25, 2009, Motown Records founder Berry Gordy released a statement on the Motown Web site:

As a kid, Michael was always beyond his years. He had a knowingness about him that was incredible. . . .

Somehow, even at that first meeting with him, he had a hunger to learn, a hunger to be the best and was willing to work as hard and as long as it took.

I had no concern about his ability to go to the top. He was like my son. He had warmth, sensitivity and two personalities.

When he was not on stage, he was loving, respectful and shy. When he WAS on stage, he was so in charge you would not believe he was the same person.

Michael was and will remain one of the greatest entertainers that ever lived.

He was exceptional, artistic and original. He gave the world his heart and soul through his music.[1]

▲ MICHAEL JACKSON'S LEGACY INCLUDES HIS RECORD-BREAKING *THRILLER* ALBUM.

album, *Bad*. Sadly, Jackson's personal life often overshadowed his musical achievements during the 27 years following the release of the mega-selling *Thriller* album. His appearance, his interaction with children, his finances, his marriages, his pets, his reclusive lifestyle, and his eccentric habits made headlines over the years. Yet, through all this, Jackson remained a performer. He had been rehearsing and planning for his sold-out comeback tour in 2009.

His influence as a musician is evident in many of the musical stars who have risen in the years since Jackson first took the stage. Their styles, showmanship, videos, and professionalism all speak to Jackson's enduring legacy. Many successful performers note Jackson as an influence upon their work.

On June 25, 2009, Jim Henke, vice president of exhibitions and curatorial affairs at the Rock and Roll Hall of Fame and Museum issued a statement. He talked about Jackson's mark on the musical world: "Few other artists of his era reached the peaks that he did, both in terms of sales and critical acclaim. His legacy will live on for a long, long time."[2]

"Ever since I was born, daddy has been the best father you could ever imagine. And I just want to say that I love him so much."[3]
—*Paris Michael Katherine Jackson, at Jackson's memorial service*

▲ MICHAEL JACKSON MADE HIS MARK AND GAINED COUNTLESS FANS WITH HIS "THRILLER" VIDEO.

TIMELINE

1958

Michael Jackson is born in Gary, Indiana, on August 29.

1967

The Jackson 5 wins amateur night competition at Apollo Theater in Harlem on August 13.

1969

The Jackson 5 releases its debut album, *Diana Ross Presents the Jackson 5,* in December.

1982

Jackson releases the album *Thriller* on December 1.

1983

Jackson performs on the *Motown 25: Yesterday, Today and Forever* TV special, broadcast on May 16.

1983

In December, MTV debuts Jackson's 14-minute music video for the "Thriller" single.

1971

Jackson's first solo album, *Got To Be There*, is released in November.

1979

The album *Off The Wall* is released in August.

1979

In February, Jackson wins a Grammy for Best R & B Vocal Performance, Male.

1984

Jackson wins eight Grammys.

1985

Jackson helps gather musicians to record "We Are the World" to raise money for famine relief in Africa.

1987

Jackson releases his album *Bad* on October 1.

TIMELINE

1989

Jackson completes his first solo tour.

1991

Jackson releases his album *Dangerous*.

1993

Jackson is accused of assaulting a boy but is not arrested.

2001

Jackson is inducted into the Rock and Roll Hall of Fame as a solo artist.

2001

Jackson releases *Invincible*, his last album.

2003

Police arrest and charge Jackson with assault.

1995

Jackson releases *HIStory: Past, Present, and Future.*

1997

The Jackson 5 is inducted into the Rock and Roll Hall of Fame.

1997

Jackson releases his album *Blood on the Dance Floor.*

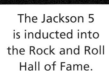

2005

On June 14, a jury acquits Jackson of all charges related to his alleged assault on a boy.

2009

In March, Jackson announces a series of 50 final concerts to be held in London.

2009

Jackson dies in Los Angeles from cardiac arrest on June 25.

QUICK FACTS

DATE OF BIRTH
August 29, 1958

PLACE OF BIRTH
Gary, Indiana

DATE OF DEATH
June 25, 2009

PLACE OF DEATH
Los Angeles, California

PARENTS
Joseph and Katherine Jackson

MARRIAGE
Lisa Marie Presley (1994–1996)
Deborah Rowe (1996–1999)

CHILDREN
Prince Michael Joseph Jackson (1997)
Paris Michael Katherine Jackson (1998)
Prince Michael Joseph "Blanket" Jackson II (2002)

IMPORTANT WORKS

Group Albums
Diana Ross Presents the Jackson 5 (1969)
ABC (1970)
The Jacksons (1976)

Solo Albums
Got To Be There (1971)
Off The Wall (1979)
Thriller (1982)
Bad (1987)
Dangerous (1991)
HIStory: Past, Present, and Future (1995)
Blood on the Dance Floor (1997)
Invincible (2001)

Other Albums
E.T.: The Extra Terrestrial (1983)

Film
The Wiz (1977)

Book
Moonwalk (1988)

QUOTE

"Few other artists of his era reached the peaks that he did, both in terms of sales and critical acclaim. His legacy will live on for a long, long time."—*Jim Henke, vice president of exhibitions and curatorial affairs at the Rock and Roll Hall of Fame and Museum*

ADDITIONAL RESOURCES

SELECT BIBLIOGRAPHY

Anderson, Christopher. *Michael Jackson Unauthorized.* New York: Simon & Schuster, 1994.

Brooks, Darren. *Michael Jackson An Exceptional Journey: The Unauthorized Biography in Words and Pictures.* New Malden, Surrey, Eng.: Chrome Dreams, 2002.

Jackson, Michael. *Moonwalk.* New York: Doubleday, 1988.

Nicholson, Lois P. *Michael Jackson Entertainer.* New York: Chelsea House, 1994.

FURTHER READING

Jefferson, Margo. *On Michael Jackson.* New York: Pantheon Books, 2006.

Life Commemorative: Michael Jackson. Spec. issue of *Life Magazine.* 2009.

Taraborrelli, J. Randy. *Michael Jackson: The Magic and the Madness.* New York: Birch Lane, 1991.

WEB LINKS

To learn more about Michael Jackson, visit ABDO Publishing Company online at **www.abdopublishing.com**. Web sites about Michael Jackson are featured on our Book Links page. These links are routinely monitored and updated to provide the most current information available.

FOR MORE INFORMATION

For more information on this subject, contact or visit the following organizations.

Essential Michael Jackson Coverage

Rolling Stone Magazine Online
www.rollingstone.com/news/story/28852664/
rolling_stones_essential_michael_jackson_coverage
Rolling Stone magazine's Web site has a Michael Jackson Web page with links to a variety of Jackson-related information, including news stories, photos, and album reviews.

Michael Jackson Remembered

MTV Web site
www.mtv.com/specials/michaeljackson
The MTV Web page devoted to Michael Jackson includes links to many of his videos and footage of celebrities sharing what they remember of Michael Jackson.

Rock and Roll Hall of Fame and Museum

751 Erieside Avenue, Cleveland, OH 44114
216-781-ROCK (7625)
www.rockhall.com
The Rock and Roll Hall of Fame has exhibits and collections commemorating musicians and events in rock and roll history. The museum also has information about all inductees, including Michael Jackson.

GLOSSARY

addiction
    A desire for something that cannot be controlled or easily stopped.

album
    A collection of recorded songs.

autobiography
    A book that someone writes about himself or herself.

Billboard
    A weekly magazine about the music industry.

compensation
    Payment for work done.

contract
    A document or agreement that states the terms of working together.

controversial
    Something that causes people to argue or disagree.

disclaimer
    A statement that denies responsibility for something.

en pointe
    A French term from ballet that means going up on one's toes.

groom
    To teach another person how to act and think.

groundbreaking
 Something new and different.

Jehovah's Witnesses
 A Christian religion.

legendary
 To be famous or well known.

lineup
 A list of players or people taking part in an activity.

mentor
 A teacher or adviser.

negotiate
 To discuss and agree with another person.

phenomenon
 A rare and unusual event, person, or thing.

plastic surgery
 Surgery to alter a person's body or face.

prosperity
 Being very successful, particularly being successful with money.

single
 One song.

solo
 One person, or an action done by one person.

SOURCE NOTES

Chapter 1. A Dazzling Performer
1. "Billie Jean," *Rolling Stone Special Commemorative Issue Michael Jackson 1958–2009*. 2009. 76.
2. Michael Jackson. *Moonwalk*. New York: Doubleday, 1988. 191.
3. Ibid. 217.
4. Ibid.
5. Ibid. 122.
6. Lois P. Nicholson. *Michael Jackson Entertainer*. New York: Chelsea House, 1994. 14.
7. Michael Jackson. *Moonwalk*. New York: Doubleday, 1988. 213.

Chapter 2. Growing Up Jackson
1. Michael Jackson. *Moonwalk*. New York: Doubleday, 1988. 26.
2. Ibid. 6.
3. Ibid. 19.
4. Christopher Anderson. *Michael Jackson Unauthorized*. New York: Simon & Schuster, 1994. 28.

Chapter 3. The Rise of the Jackson 5
1. Michael Jackson. *Moonwalk*. New York: Doubleday, 1988. 17.
2. Ibid. 67.
3. Ibid. 29.
4. Lauren Sher and Chris Connelly. "Controversial Father Joe Jackson Speaks Out on the Making of Superstar Son, Exclusive: Inside the Jackson Compound, and the Tumultuous Father-Son Relationship." *ABC News Online*. 14 July 2009. 16 Aug. 2009 <http://abcnews. go.com/Primetime/MichaelJackson/Story?id=8072081&page=1>.
5. Paul Harris and Jo Clements. "Michael Jackson 'took revenge on years of abuse by his father' by cutting him out of his will." *Mail Online*. London, July 1, 2009. <http://www.dailymail.co.uk/news/article-1196695/Michael-Jackson-took-revenge-years-abuse-father-cutting-will.html>.

Chapter 4. The Jackson 5 Era

1. Michael Jackson. *Moonwalk*. New York: Doubleday, 1988. 67.
2. Ibid. 13.
3. Ibid. 9.
4. J. Randy Taraborrelli. *Michael Jackson: The Magic and the Madness*. New York: Carol Publishing, 1991. 42.
5. Michael Jackson. *Moonwalk*. New York: Doubleday, 1988. 99.
6. Ibid. 90.
7. Ibid. 87.
8. J. Randy Taraborrelli. *Michael Jackson: The Magic and the Madness*. New York: Carol Publishing, 1991. 153.

Chapter 5. Going Solo

1. J. Randy Taraborrelli. *Michael Jackson: The Magic and the Madness*. New York: Carol Publishing, 1991. 206.
2. Michael Jackson. *Moonwalk*. New York: Doubleday, 1988. 155.
3. Anthony DeCurtis. "Off the Wall: Michael Reinvents Pop." *Rolling Stone Special Commemorative Issue Michael Jackson 1958–2009*. 2009. 44.
4. J. Randy Taraborrelli. *Michael Jackson: The Magic and the Madness*. New York: Carol Publishing, 1991. 231.
5. Michael Jackson. *Moonwalk*. New York: Doubleday, 1988. 164.
6. J. Randy Taraborrelli. *Michael Jackson: The Magic and the Madness*. New York: Carol Publishing, 1991. 233.

Chapter 6. *Thriller*

1. Michael Jackson. *Moonwalk*. New York: Doubleday, 1988. 180.
2. Christopher Connelly. "Michael Jackson Thriller Album Review." *Rolling Stone Online*. 28 Jan. 1983. 16 Aug. 2009 <http://www.rollingstone.com/artists/michaeljackson/albums/album/303823/review/6067536/thriller>.
3. Michael Jackson. *Moonwalk*. New York: Doubleday, 1988. 200.

SOURCE NOTES
CONTINUED

4. Gail Mitchell and Melinda Newman. "Exclusive: How Michael Jackson's 'Thriller' Changed the Music Business." *Billboard.com*. 3 July 2009. 16 Aug. 2009 <http://www.billboard.com/bbcom/news/exclusive-how-michael-jackson-s-thriller-1003990525.story#/bbcom/news/exclusive-how-michael-jackson-s-thriller-1003990525.story>.
5. Rob Sheffield. "A New Kind of Hollywood Musical." *Rolling Stone Special Commemorative Issue Michael Jackson 1958–2009*. 2009. 74.
6. Michael Jackson. *Moonwalk*. New York: Doubleday, 1988. 238.
7. Gail Mitchell and Melinda Newman. "Exclusive: How Michael Jackson's 'Thriller' Changed the Music Business." *Billboard.com*. 3 July 2009. 16 Aug. 2009 <http://www.billboard.com/bbcom/news/exclusive-how-michael-jackson-s-thriller-1003990525.story#/bbcom/news/exclusive-how-michael-jackson-s-thriller-1003990525.story>.

Chapter 7. A Life of Fame
1. Michael Jackson. *Moonwalk*. New York: Doubleday, 1988. 262.
2. Davitt Sigerson. "Michael Jackson Bad Album Review." *Rolling Stone Online*. 22 Oct. 1987. 16 Aug. 2009 <http://www.rollingstone.com/reviews/album/259584/review/6067877/bad>.
3. Michael Jackson. *Moonwalk*. New York: Doubleday, 1988. 270.
4. Ibid.
5. Ibid. n. pag.
6. Darren Brooks. *Michael Jackson An Exceptional Journey: The Unauthorized Biography in Words and Pictures*. New Malden, Surrey, Eng.: Chrome Dreams, 2002. 57.

Chapter 8. Marriage, Family, and Controversy
1. Lisa Marie Presley. "He Knew." *Lisa Marie Presley's MySpace Page*. 26 June 2009. 16 Aug 2009 <http://www.facebook.com/topic.php?uid=95311679543&topic=8193>.
2. Linda Deutsch. "Ex-wife praises Jackson at trial: Says he fell victim to opportunists." *Boston Globe Online*. 29 Apr. 2005. 16 Aug. 2009

<http://www.boston.com/news/nation/articles/2005/04/29/ex_wife_praises_jackson_at_trial/>.

3. "Jackson leaving the US behind." *Boston Globe Online*. 10 Nov. 2005. 16 Aug. 2009 <http://www.boston.com/news/globe/living/articles/2005/11/10/jackson_leaving_the_us_behind/>.

4. Daniel Kreps. "Michael Jackson Announces 10-Concert Run at London's O2 Arena." *Rolling Stone Online*. 5 Mar. 2009. 16 Aug. 2009 <http://www.rollingstone.com/rockdaily/index.php/2009/03/05/michael jackson-announces-ten-concert-run-at-londons-o2-arena/#>.

5. Martin Bashir. "Michael Jackson, the Greatest Entertainer Has Died: *Nightline* Co-Anchor Reflects on Eight Months Documenting Jackson on Neverland Ranch." *ABC News.com*. 25 June 2009. 16 Aug. 2009 <http://abcnews.go.com/Entertainment/MichaelJackson/story?id=7933530&page=1>.

Chapter 9. Dead at 50

1. Berry Gordy. "Berry Gordy Statement on the passing of Michael Jackson." *Motown.com*. 25 June 2009. 26 Aug. 2009 <http://www.motown.com/>.

2. Jim Henke. "Michael Jackson." Rock and Roll Hall of Fame and Museum. 25 June 2009. 26 Aug. 2009 <http://www.rockhall.com/inductee/michael-jackson>.

3. Alan Duke and Saeed Ahmed. "Goodbye Michael Jackson: Star, brother, friend, father." *CNN.com*. 26 Aug. 2009 <http://www.cnn.com/2009/SHOWBIZ/Music/07/07/michael.jackson.wrap/>.

INDEX

 ABOUT THE AUTHOR

Mary K. Pratt is a journalist based in Massachusetts. Pratt worked as a staff newspaper reporter for a decade, where she covered community news, health and fitness topics, business issues, and fashion. As a freelancer, she has written for a variety of publications, including newspapers, magazines, and trade journals. Much of her recent work has focused on business and information technology. When not working, Pratt enjoys spending time with her family and pursuing outdoor activities, such as swimming and hiking.

 PHOTO CREDITS

Alan Greth/AP Images, cover, 3, 73, 98; NBC/Photofest, 7; Shaan Kokin/AP Images, 10, 57; AP Images, 13, 17, 21, 25, 31, 43, 45, 49, 55, 70, 75, 81, 82; Epic Records/Photofest, 15, 93; Photofest, 19, 35, 37, 47, 77; Dima Gavrysh/AP Images, 27, 96 (top); Charles Rex Arbogast/AP Images, 40, 97; Dan Steinberg/AP Images, 53; Yui Mok/AP Images, 61; MCA/Universal Home Video/Photofest, 63, 95; Isaac Sutton/ AP Images, 65, 96 (bottom); Luca Bruno/AP Images, 67, 99 (top); Joel Ryan/AP Images, 85, 99 (bottom); Wally Skalij/AP Images, 87; Shoun A. Hill/AP Images, 89; Mark J. Terrill/AP Images, 91